# The Coach drivers Cookbook.

### Recipes from my travels and more.

S. Gaiger.

# Introduction.

Being a coach driver exposed me to some amazing dishes from all over the U.K. and Europe. With a love of food and trying new, local recipes I have over the years gathered knowledge of the little tricks that chefs use to make these wonderful plates of food.

Growing up we never had much, food was never really exciting. As kids our highlight of the week was Sunday roast (always Chicken) and a takeaway was rare, consisting of a visit to the local Chinese for Chicken and Chips.

Never being taught to cook it was only when I moved out of my parents that I had to learn, with many disasters on the way. Cooking programs on the T.V. were my inspiration and I learned what ingredients went together.

Fast forwarding many years and my love for food, travel and cooking has exploded into a vast array of favourite plates of scrummy goodness.

Many of the dishes in this book have been adapted over time, some are easy versions of popular classics which can be knocked up in the smallest of kitchens with a minimum amount of time and hassle. A few are more accomplished but still achievable by the novice home cook. A few have been handed down by family members, local chefs in the hotels I have visited and also my own creations/ adaptations. They are mainly based on ingredients that can be found in your cupboards and fridges (a few require more specialised ingredients), herbs and spices are used a lot in my recipes, I use a lot of fresh herbs but these can be substituted with dried versions easily.

Cooking and personal taste is always an individual thing, I generally don't use exact measures (only in certain dishes do they matter) but tend to use splashes, glugs and pinches. The important thing is to taste along the way and add a splash more or an extra pinch along the way until it satisfies your palette, you can always add ingredients but it is much harder to backtrack if you chuck too much in to start with!

I make no apology for using some packet mixes, there is a great array of easy and ready prepared items to make life easier, and sometimes when time is tight using a packet mix for things like pastry or a cheese sauce etc… can be invaluable to get a tasty and filling meal on the table. I use a lot of Extra virgin olive oil as I find it enhances the flavour of sauces and is better than vegetable or sunflower oil. You can use other oil if that is all you have to hand.

This book hopefully inspires home cooks to try something new and get the pots and pans rattling!


Happy cooking, Steve.

# Contents.

# Accompaniments

Sometimes meals need a tasty accompaniment, whether it's a roast dinner or a salad. This section provides a few "extras" that are quick and simple to make but will add an extra dimension to your food.

## Simple Italian salad dressing.

It is no secret that Italians love their salad, always very fresh produce, not complicated but so tasty. To give it a lift they always add a dressing (either plain olive oil (extra virgin of course) or something with an extra bite) this dressing is my take on the flavour of Italy.

Ingredients.

1 clove of garlic

1 small sweet red pepper

Fresh parsley (flat leaf)

Fresh basil

Extra virgin olive oil (1st press)

Balsamic vinegar

Salt & pepper (I use rock salt and mixed peppercorns)

In a bowl put a good slug of olive oil (approx. 5 tablespoons) add 2 teaspoons of balsamic vinegar.

Peel the garlic and crush with the blade of a kitchen knife, then finely chop (use a garlic press if you have one) and add to the bowl, finely dice the red pepper (removing the seeds and white fleshy middle bit) and add to your mixture. Roughly chop the parsley and basil (including the stalks) and add, follow with a fresh grind of salt & pepper. Stir everything together and leave for 10mins to allow the flavours to mix, then just drizzle over your salad using a spoon.

N.B. if you possess a food blender (like I do) you can just throw all the ingredients in whole (apart from the red pepper which needs to be de-seeded first) and whizz until blended.

## Tip:

When selecting olive oil always buy one in a glass bottle, whilst visiting an olive oil producer in Tuscany they explained that plastic bottles causes the oil to degrade quickly and affects the taste and life of the product.

## Easy potato salad.

Whether you are making a fresh salad or looking for something to add as a side dish there is nothing like a homemade potato salad. This recipe takes very little time to make but will keep in the fridge for 3-4 days and is much nicer than shop bought versions.

Ingredients.

New potatoes (jersey royals if available)

Dijon mustard (Colemans is too intense in heat)

1 Spring onion

Mayonnaise

½ lemon

Salt & pepper


Boil the potatoes until your knife just goes in without too much pressure, then drain and set aside until cooled down.

Once cold, slice the potatoes (skin still on) and place in a bowl. Chop the spring onion and add to the bowl, add 1 teaspoon of mustard, a small pinch of salt & pepper and the zest of ½ lemon, then squirt on the mayo. Stir until all the potato is covered in the mixture and then cover and place in the fridge.

And there you have it! Simple to make yet so tasty!

Note:

If you can't get spring onions, then you can use chopped chives. Adding chopped coriander will also give a little extra zing

The lemon zest can be left out if you don't have one to hand.

# Easy naan bread.

Everybody knows that a curry often comes with a flat bread, as most of us don't possess a tikka oven to cook them with the pre-made ones in the supermarket seem like the only option. Here is a recipe to make your own easily and quickly.

## Ingredients.

Self-raising flour

Natural Greek yoghurt

Salt & pepper

In a bowl put the yoghurt, a pinch of salt & pepper and stir together, then slowly add flour mixing all the time until you reach a consistency that resembles playdough. Take a lump of the mixture and with your hands manipulate it into a flat-ish round shape (approx.1/2 the thickness of your thumb).

On a hob place a frying pan (griddle pan if you have one) and heat up at a fairly high temperature, place the flat bread into the dry pan and cook for a couple of minutes before turning over, cook until it starts to brown turning every couple of mins then serve brushing with a tiny amount of olive oil.

Note.

Using garlic paste in the mixture before cooking also adds an extra dimension.

It is also possible, once cooked to carefully slice down the length of the bread making a pocket to fill with whatever takes your fancy (a simple pita-bread).

# Doug's delicious stuffing.

We all know that a roast deserves to have a nice tasty stuffing to accompany it!

Shop bought stuffing mixes are ok, but I find they can be grainy and dry. I like a nice moist stuffing with a crispy crust on the top, full of flavour and rich in texture.

This recipe was passed to me by my late brother-in-law and I have used it ever since, so this one is for you Doug!

## Ingredients.

Salted butter

Olive oil

1 medium onion

Dried mixed herbs

Salt & pepper

White (or brown) bread

Melt 1/3 block of butter in a saucepan with a small slug of olive oil, dice the onion into small chunks and gently fry until see through (don't let them brown) then add a generous handful of the mixed herbs, a pinch of salt & pepper and stir together. Turn the heat down low to keep the mixture warm but not to continue frying the onions.

Cut the crusts off the bread and then chop the slices into squares, slowly add the bread to the saucepan stirring it in until all the liquid has been absorbed but remains moist.

Transfer the mixture into an ovenproof dish and set aside, approx. 20mins before you wish to serve place the stuffing onto the middle shelf of your oven at 180'c (no idea of the gas mark! Don't have gas!) you will know when it's done as the top will have a nice brown crispy crust.

Note.

You could roll the mixture into balls if you wish, but the mixture would have to be cooled first then placed on a baking tray to finish off.

The crusts can be saved and broken down to make breadcrumbs with.

# Luscious lamb chops and a red wine sauce.

Lamb is one of my favourite meats to cook with, and nothing beats fresh welsh lamb! Chops from a supermarket are fine but I get mine from a local butcher and the difference in taste and quality is amazing!

Ingredients.

Lamb chops

Olive oil

Red wine (I use a merlot but whatever you have will do)

Mushrooms

Fresh parsley

2 shallots (1 small red onion would do)

1 small sweet red pepper

1 lamb stock pot (I use Knorr stock pots)

Fresh rosemary

Fresh thyme

Peas (tinned garden, frozen whatever you have)

New potatoes

Salt & pepper

Butter

I like to marinade my chops for at least an hour before starting to cook them, for that I place the chops in a bowl then add a slug of red wine, a glug of olive oil, fresh rosemary and fresh thyme, finally a fresh grind of salt and pepper. Cover the bowl and set aside in the fridge.

In a frying pan melt some butter, take the lamb and gently fry in the butter for 3-4 mins per side before putting on a baking tray in a pre-heated oven at 160'c for 8-10mins (depending on how pink you like your meat) don't forget you need to rest the lamb before serving.

Meanwhile in the frying pan add the shallots (finely chopped) and cook until translucent, then add sliced mushrooms, finely diced red pepper and the liquid from the marinade. Add another good glug of red wine and the stock pot along with roughly chopped fresh parsley. Turn up the heat to allow the sauce to reduce by at least ½. The more the liquid reduces the more intense the flavour, add salt and pepper to taste.

I serve mine with boiled new parsley potatoes and petit pois, but they could be served with a creamy mash or whatever you like.

Always a crowd pleaser and very easy to cook, this recipe allows you to produce really tasty food that looks amazing, smells divine and tastes like you were in a top restaurant!

# Fish cakes.

These fishcakes take a while to prepare but are so worth it. Also once made you can freeze the ones you don't use straight away and then there will be some ready to cook whenever you want in the future! I like to serve with a nice cauliflower cheese (recipe found later in the book) and a side salad with fresh dressing (see first section for the dressing)

Ingredients.

Smoked haddock)

Salmon             ) – you can easily use a fish pie mix from a supermarket

Cod                 ) to save time dicing and de-boning the fish

4-5 large Potatoes

Cheddar cheese

Spring onion

Breadcrumbs

2-3 eggs whisked

Plain flour

Milk

Butter

Fresh parsley

Fresh dill

Salt & pepper

Peel and chop the potatoes into large chunks and boil them until soft (so a knife slides in easily) then drain the water away. Using a couple of knobs of butter, mash the potatoes taking care not to make it too creamy. (the mash needs to be quite dry at this point) add a pinch of salt & pepper to season the mash. Put into a bowl and allow to stand and cool down.

In a large shallow pan (frying pan would do) put a knob of butter, dice the fish into similar sized chunks (taking out any bones) and place in the pan, pour in milk until the fish is just covered add roughly chopped parsley and dill. Gently poach the fish on a low temperature so as not to burn the milk.

When the salmon changes colour to a pale pink take the pan off the heat (about 5mins), strain off the liquid into a jug through a sieve leaving just the fish and herbs. Put to one side to cool.

Once the potatoes and fish are cool, add them together along with chopped spring onion and grated cheddar (how much depends on how cheesy you want them to be) then it's time to get messy …. Get your hands in the mixture and thoroughly mix all the ingredients together, flaking the fish apart as you go so that it is evenly distributed throughout.

Place the flour, egg and breadcrumbs in separate bowls, take a tablespoon of the mixture (more if you want bigger fishcakes) and in your hands mould them into the shape you want (round, square, triangle …. Get creative!). then with your cake place first in the flour until it is covered, then into the egg mixture (you need to be quite quick otherwise the fishcake goes soggy and falls apart) and finally the breadcrumbs, making sure the whole surface is covered. Place on greaseproof paper and repeat until all the mixture is used up.

For those you wish to cook on the same day place on a plate (cover with cling film) and in the fridge to firm up for about 30mins. Any fishcakes you wish to freeze, wrap them individually and place in a freezer bag/ plastic tub and put them in the freezer.

When it's time to cook them, place a little oil in a frying pan (can be any oil you want) and gently fry the fishcakes until they are golden brown on both sides, serve with your chosen accompaniment and enjoy the cheesy, fishy goodness!

Note.

It is possible to oven cook the fishcakes if you wish to, cutting out the need for the oil, I would do this at 160'-180'c until golden brown.

The saved cooking liquor from the fish can be used to make a cream sauce to accompany your meal (simply reheat, add cheese and cream and serve)

# Steve's steak and Guinness pie.

Who doesn't like a good pub lunch from time to time? And there is nothing that says pub lunch more than a good old steak & ale pie! This is one of my favourites and I have tried many ways of cooking the filling to arrive at what I think is the richest and most opulent pie you will ever taste. For the pastry I use a bit of a cheat, by using a packet mix, I just add water and mix, then roll out … although I buy mine in large bags at a wholesaler's all major supermarkets sell shortcrust pastry mix.

Ingredients.

Pack of diced beef (stewing steak would be fine)

1 can Guinness

1 red onion

Rich beef stock pot

1 clove of garlic (or garlic paste would do)

Mushrooms

Cornflour (for thickening)

Mixed herbs (I use dried herbs de province for this recipe)

Flour

1 egg

Salt & pepper

Shortcrust pastry (packet mix, ready rolled)

In a pan, add a small splash of oil, roughly chop the onion and add to the pan, finely chop the garlic and add along with a good shake of the mixed herbs. Slice the mushrooms and add. Then add the full can of Guinness and the stock cube, allow to simmer adding a pinch of salt & pepper. In a frying pan drizzle a splash of oil, trim all the fat off of the steak then roll in flour before frying it off to seal the meat, keep turning the steak until it is browned on all sides (do this a little at a time rather than all in one go) then add it to your saucepan with the gravy in.

Leave the pan to simmer for about 45 mins stirring occasionally, allowing the beef to soak up all the flavour and the gravy to reduce (and hopefully thicken). Then take the pan off the heat, if the gravy needs thickening use a teaspoon of cornflower (or bisto) and stir in thoroughly. Set aside to allow the filling to cool.

This is where it gets a little tricky (until you have done it once or twice), make up the pastry (as instructed on the packet) or unroll it if you are using pre-made.

If you are making the pastry, you need to roll it out, so it is no thinner than a teaspoon handle. (make sure you have enough for the top of the pie as well). Line your pie tin/ ovenproof dish (whatever you are using) with the pastry being careful not to split it, tucking it in all the corners and leaving a lip over the top to seal your lid to.

Place over the top some greaseproof paper and weight down with baking beads (if you don't have them, use what you have to hand) blind bake the case in a pre-heated oven 160'c for 10mins then remove.

Take out the beads and paper to reveal your pie case, fill with your filling then place over the top your lid sealing it down by brushing egg wash on the edges. Brush the lid with the egg and make a small slice with a knife in the lid (to allow steam to escape).

Put back into the oven at 180'c for about 20 mins (or until golden brown), remove and serve!


Note.

Any leftover filling can be put into a tub and kept in the freezer for use at a later date, or if you make several pies and want to keep them in the freezer for another day this is also possible as long as they are well wrapped.

# Spinach & ricotta ravioli.

Pasta is a staple food in Italy. Every meal will have a pasta course of some sort. Making fresh pasta can seem a bit daunting to start with, but it is so easy to do and when you talk ravioli it, (in my opinion) is the only way to go.

I learned how to make pasta (without a pasta machine) in Tuscany a few years ago and this recipe is easy to follow, tastes divine and will leave you wanting more.

Ingredients.

Good quality strong plain flour (not bread flour)

2 medium eggs

Bag of baby spinach

Tub of ricotta cheese

Butter

Olive oil

Salt & pepper

First you need to make the filling so it can cool down while you make the pasta (you don't want the pasta to cook before it goes into the water). In a pan put a knob of butter and a good slug of olive oil (most cookbooks tell you to use water to wilt spinach, but I find this just makes it a bit slimy). Roughly chop up the spinach including the stalks and put into the pan on a low heat, stir until spinach has wilted (it will wilt down to a fraction of its raw size). Drain of the liquid and put aside in a bowl to cool.

Put 100g(approx. 5 heaped tablespoons) of flour into a bowl and make a well in the middle, crack 1 egg into the well. With a fork start to whisk the egg, slowly taking a small amount of the flour each time to combine with the egg. Do this until most of the flour has been incorporated, then get you hand in there and mix the last bits together, kneading the dough until it is smooth (if it seems too dry and grainy run your fingers under the cold tap and carry on mixing). Wrap the dough in clingfilm and put aside to rest, it needs to rest for about 30mins to let the gluten make the dough elastic.

Once the spinach has cooled, drain the excess water off the ricotta and add the cheese to the spinach and mix thoroughly adding a pinch of salt & pepper to season.

Put on a pot of water with plenty of salt (it needs to be as salty as seawater) and bring to the boil leaving it on a rolling boil.

Take a small piece of the pasta (about the size of a grape) and place on a lightly floured board (make sure to keep the rest of the dough wrapped up to stop it drying out) and with a rolling pin start to roll out the dough, turning it over frequently and rolling in all directions until the dough is wafer thin. Cut the finished pasta into wide rectangles approx. 2inches wide and 4inches long, take a teaspoon of the filling and place into the centre of your pasta, brush around the edge of ½ the remaining pasta, fold together to make a seal, trim off any excess pasta to tidy it up (leaving a lip ) press down gently with the back of a fork to ensure the seam of the ravioli is sealed.

Repeat the process for all the pasta and filling (you can save it for another day if you store it in the fridge)

One by one drop the ravioli into the boiling water with a serving spoon and leave to cook, you will know when they are ready because they will float to the top of the pan, if you are not sure, lift one out and pinch the corner with your finger, it will feel soft and slippery. And there you have it! Spinach and ricotta ravioli!!

I serve mine with a side salad drizzled with either plain olive oil or the dressing found at the beginning of this book.

Note.

The filling could be anything you fancy, a bolognaise sauce, ham and cheese, pesto … the process for the pasta is the same!

# Beef & black pudding burgers.

Anyone who knows me will understand how much I love a good burger!

I first experienced a black pudding burger in a garden café in Scotland and I never found another to come even close … so I now make my own! And I'd like to share my recipe with you!

Ingredients.

500g good quality mince beef (at least 10% fat content)

150g black pudding

1 red onion

Fresh parsley

Finely chop the red onion and parsley, remove the outer skin of the black pudding and dice into small chunks. Empty all the ingredients including the mince into a bowl and thoroughly mix with your hands.

I use a burger press for the next bit, (available in the range for about £6) but you can use any flat hard surface and the bottom of a plate/ saucepan etc…

Take a tablespoon of the mince mixture and shape into a burger patty, make sure that the ingredients are as tightly packed together as physically possible. Place in the fridge to chill before cooking.

Extras can be frozen for a later date.

And that's it! Serve in a brioche bun, with salad leaves, cheese, fried onion and there you have it, a tasty and meaty burger with a kick!

# Sylvana's tomato, pesto, cream & brandy pasta sauce.

On one of my many visits to Diano Marina in Italy, the hotel served up this pasta dish. It was so tasty that I asked the chef for the recipe, which she was happy to share. On returning home I got the pots and pans out to re-create this unique and tasty pasta dish. I use dried packet pasta for this as it seems to hold together better than fresh pasta.

The secret to making this sauce is a little time and patience.

This one is dedicated to Sylvana of the hotel Nettuno.

Ingredients.

2 tins of chopped plum tomatoes

1 medium onion

1 clove garlic

Double cream

1 jar pesto

Olive oil

1 double shot of brandy

Salt & pepper

Pasta of your choice (I use penne or rigatoni)

Finely chop the onion and add to a pan along with a glug of olive oil and crushed garlic, lightly fry until soft then add the tins of tomatoes, stir and then place a lid on the pan, turning the heat down low to simmer for about an hour. Keep stirring the tomato mixture to stop it sticking to the pan (as time goes on, the tomatoes get sweeter and loose their tanginess).

Now add the brandy and pesto stirring it into your sauce, add salt & pepper to taste.

Boil your pasta until it is not quite soft and floppy (it should have a little bite to it!) then drain.

Always add the pasta to the sauce, never the other way round! Just before adding the pasta, tip a good slug of cream to your sauce and mix, adding the pasta keep stirring until it is all covered in the sauce.

Serve and enjoy, if you like, grate some parmesan over the top but I don't think personally it is needed!

# Easy Spaghetti bolognaise

There is nothing quite like a good old spag-bol, everybody knows the struggle of getting the spaghetti on your fork, then sucking that one strand up and flicking a bit of sauce up your nose, in your eye etc… it travels at a huge velocity! Here is my easy but tasty and fresh bolognaise sauce.

Ingredients.

500g Beef mince (at least 10% fat)

1 tin peeled chopped plum tomatoes

Tomato puree or passata

2 cloves garlic

1 medium red onion

Fresh basil

Olive oil

1 teaspoon paprika

1 red pepper

Fresh parsley

Salt & pepper

Parmesan

Dried spaghetti

In a pan add a drizzle of oil, then finely chop the onion and garlic and add to the pan, fry them for 1-2 mins until they are starting to soften.

 Add the mince and stir until it has all browned.

De-seed the pepper and dice into small pieces and add to the pan along with the tomatoes. Stir in well, chop the basil and add to the mix along with a pinch of salt & pepper.

Allow to simmer for ½ hour stirring often to make sure the bolognaise is cooked right through and doesn't stick to the pan. Meanwhile boil a pan of salted water then add the spaghetti, cook until it is soft, and floppy then drain into a colander.

Back to the bolognaise, squirt in a good squeeze of tomato puree and mix in, finely chop some parsley and add together with the spaghetti. (always add pasta to sauce never the other way round) stir thoroughly until all the pasta is covered in sauce and serve. Garnish with a sprinkling of fresh parsley and grated parmesan.

Note.

Although it is easy to make fresh garlic bread, the shop bought ones are perfectly good and only take a couple of mins in the oven to warm up.

If you do want to make fresh garlic bread, I use a part-bake baguette, slice diagonally across the top several times to make slices being careful not to cut all the way through. In a bowl take a large knob of butter, crushed garlic cloves and finely cut chives, mix together thoroughly to make a garlic butter. Spread the butter in-between each of the cuts you made in the baguette and place in the oven to finish the cooking process of the bread.

# Cottage pie.

Shepherds pie/ cottage pie, there is a difference between the two, one is cooked with beef mince and one is lamb mince. Either way the basic principle is the same, meat, gravy and mash!

Here is my easy version with a great little tip to stop the mash from sinking into the gravy too much.

Ingredients.

Potatoes

Cheddar cheese

Butter

1 egg

Milk

Mince (lamb, beef even turkey would work (low fat content under 10%)

1 onion

1 rich beef/lamb stock pot

1 tin of garden peas

1 tin of baby carrots

Oxo cubes

Bisto

Mixed herbs

Salt & pepper

In a pan place a knob of butter, finely dice the onion and add to the pan along with a good tablespoon of the dried herbs.

Add to the pan the mince and cook off until it has browned all over, stirring all the time to combine the mince with the onions. Add ½ cup of water and crumble in 1 oxo cube, add a good pinch of salt and pepper and mix in well.

Add the peas and carrots and a full cup of water along with the stock pot. Once all of the ingredients have been allowed to simmer for 20mins, slowly add bisto 1 teaspoon full at a time until the gravy thickens so that when you stir it you can very briefly see the bottom of the pan.

Transfer to an oven dish with enough of the gravy to just be visible over the top of the mince. Finally sprinkle over the top 1 oxo cube and a light covering of bisto and leave to one side to cool.

This allows a very thin film of the gravy to form on the top of the meat so when you put the mash on top, it will not sink! (good tip eh?)

Now is the time to make the mash, peel and boil the potatoes until soft, then drain all the water out. Add a dash of milk, a good knob of butter, salt & pepper and the egg to the potatoes and mash together. The egg helps to bind it together and makes it creamy and silky smooth.

Using 2 tablespoons carefully spoon the mash on top of your cooled mince, start with a spoon at each corner, then go around in a clockwise direction working from the edges into the middle, with the back of the spoon smooth over the top of the mash to make sure all the mince is covered.

Grate a generous amount of the cheese over the top of the mash and place in a pre-heated oven at 180'c for approx. 25 mins until the top has turned brown and crispy.

And there it is, an easy cottage pie that can be served on its own or with extra veg, salad …. Whatever you fancy!


Note.

I always make a large one, once it is cooked and cooled down, I portion what is left into plastic (Chinese takeaway) tubs and store in the fridge for the next day. All it needs then is to be put on a plate and chuck it in the microwave for 3 mins …. Instant dinner!!

# German goulash soup.

Anyone who has been to Germany or Austria would have probably had this staple soup, everywhere does it slightly different but essentially it is a flavourful beefy, peppery rich soup usually served with a strong rye bread.

One of my favourites travelling around was to be found in one of the hotels I stayed in frequently, the hotel Rheinstein in a little village along the Rhein valley called Assmanshausen. Ewe and Katja who own the hotel always had a warm welcome for us, I even spent an afternoon in the kitchen teaching Ewe how to cook cottage pie!

So, I dedicate this recipe to Ewe and Katja in Assmanshausen.

Ingredients.

500g stewing steak or venison

2 tablespoons plain flower

Vegetable oil

1 large onion (finely sliced)

2 medium carrots (peeled and diced into small chunks)

1 stick of celery (chopped into small pieces)

1 small red pepper (de-seeded and cut into small chunks)

2 cloves garlic (crushed and finely chopped)

3 tablespoons paprika

1 tablespoon caraway seeds (crushed)

Tomato puree

2 bay leaves

Mushrooms (diced into small pieces)

2 rich beef stock pots

1 litre cold water

3 potatoes (peeled and cut into small cubes)

Salt & pepper

Take the meat and trim off any fatty bits, then cut into small chunks, in a bowl put the flour, a pinch of salt & pepper and add the chunks of meat. Mix it all together so that all the meat is covered in the flour.

In a large saucepan heat a glug of the oil, add the onion, carrots, celery, red pepper and garlic, cook on a lowish heat until they start to soften (about 10mins)

In a frying pan, put a drizzle of oil, gently fry the meat (in small batches) until it goes brown, once cooked add to the saucepan.

Add to the saucepan the rest of the ingredients except the potatoes, add a good pinch of salt & pepper and stir well. Place a lid on the saucepan and simmer for about an hour (stirring occasionally) on a low heat. Then add the potatoes and cook for a further 30-45mins.

The soup should then be ready to serve, maybe with a sprig of flat leaf parsley or some soured cream (if you have any).

The amounts given will serve 4-6 people, if you want to make more, just double the ingredients.

Any excess can be frozen once cooled down and kept for a quick tasty meal when you are pressed for time!

I hope you enjoy this hearty German soup; I know all my family do!

Guten appetite!

# Sausage rolls.

A really easy recipe to make a great classic. Whether you like plain sausage rolls or pork and apple, mustard, red onion .... Whatever flavour excites your palette.

This recipe is using quality shop bought sausages and packet mix for the pastry.

<u>Ingredients.</u>

1 packet sausages (quality sausages are better, but on a budget cheap ones are ok)

1 shallot

Fresh parsley

Mustard

1 egg (beaten)

Flour

Packet mix of shortcrust pastry (ready rolled would do)

Remove the sausage meat from the skins and put into a bowl, finely chop the shallot and parsley and add to the bowl and mix thoroughly. Follow instructions on packet to make the pastry or unroll if using ready roll. Lightly dust a chopping board with flour and using a rolling pin, roll out the pastry until it is the thickness of a 10p coin. Cut the pastry into large rectangles, with a pastry brush paint a thin coating of mustard along the middle of the length of the pastry. On top of the mustard place a small amount of the meat, shaping it into a tube, then simply take the pastry on one side over the meat, and roll to meet up with the other side of the pastry, sealing the two sections together with the beaten egg. Line a baking tray with greaseproof paper, place your sausage rolls onto the tray (with the join at the bottom) then brush the remaining exposed pastry with egg. Score the top of each roll with a knife and place in a pre-heated oven 180'c for 20ish mins (or until golden brown)

# Leftovers Lamb hotpot.

This is a superb way to use up leftover Lamb from a roast dinner, and twice cooked lamb is tender and succulent, a really tasty and hearty dish!

<u>Ingredients.</u>

Leftover lamb cut off the bone

1 large leek

2 medium carrots

I tin sweetcorn

1 large parsnip

1 small swede

Mixed dried herbs

500ml water

1 lamb stock pot

1 green pepper

Potatoes

Salt & pepper


The secret to my hot pot is layers, so in a large ovenproof dish (needs to have a lid) first to go in is the leek, sliced into thin slices and includes the green leaves. Cover the whole of the bottom of your dish with the leeks.

Next to go in is the lamb, trim off any fat or hard skin and dice into bite sized chunks.

Now put in the stock pot (in one lump) and add a good pinch of salt and pepper. Then empty in the tin of sweetcorn (including liquid) and spread over the top of the Lamb equally. Now peel and thinly slice the carrot & parsnip and form layers over the whole of the dish.

Peel and dice the swede into small chunks and place on top of the layers. Next de-seed the pepper and chop into small chunks, that goes in next.

Pour over the water and allow to soak through all the veg to the bottom.

Lastly peel and thinly slice the potatoes, placing over the top of everything to form a lid, make sure that you have at least 2 layers and that the potato covers everything. Finally add a pinch of salt & pepper over the top. Place the lid on you dish.

Pre-heat the oven to 180'-190'c and put the hot-pot on the middle shelf for approx. 1 ½ hrs then check on it, the gravy should be bubbling away furiously.

Remove the lid for the last ½ hr to make the top layer of the potato turn crispy.

And there it is, leftover lamb hot pot!

Note.

If you are using fresh lamb, you will need to trim off the fat, dice it into bite sized pieces and brown it off in a frying pan before adding it to the rest of the ingredients.

# Chicken in a cream & white wine sauce.

For those that enjoy chicken, this dish is for you! A creamy, mushroom sauce flavoured with white wine and chunks of moist chicken.

This recipe can be cooked in the time it takes to boil the potatoes for a mash accompaniment, and I serve it with petit pois for a spot of colour on the plate.

Ingredients.

Chicken breast pieces

1 shallot

1 tin of sweetcorn

Mushrooms

Double cream

Butter

White wine (medium sweet (chardonnay))

Salt & pepper

Fresh parsley

Potatoes

1 tin garden peas (petit pois, marrowfat.... Whatever you like)

Peel and chop into large chunks the potatoes and put them into a saucepan and on to boil.

In a large frying pan put a large knob of butter, finely chop the shallot and add to the pan.

Trim the sinew and any fat/flesh off the chicken and cut into large chunks (too small and they will dry out in the pan) add the chunks to the onion in the pan and stir until the chicken has started to brown.

Cut the mushrooms in half then slice the halves into reasonable sized pieces, add to the chicken and tip in the tin of sweetcorn, stirring to mix all of the ingredients together.

Add a good pinch of salt & pepper, the butter in the pan should start to be soaked up by the onion, chicken & mushroom by now.

It's now time to add a generous glug of white wine (of course the quality should be tested in a glass at the same time!)

Finely chop the parsley and add to your pan, give a good stir and allow to simmer for 15-20mins.

While the chicken simmers and the wine starts to reduce, you should have time to mash your potatoes (if you are having mash), drain them of water, add a large knob of butter, salt & pepper and a little drop of the cream. Mash away to make a smooth creamy mashed pile of goodness.

While mashing the potatoes put the peas on to warm up and cook through.

Just before serving add a good quantity of cream and stir into your chicken, making sure it is all coated with the sauce.

Serve onto a plate and don't forget to spoon plenty of the sauce with the chicken.

# Chicken curry.

Most people like a good curry, whether it is a Chinese, Indian, Thai, Jamaican or many other variations. the fact is we are a nation of curry lovers. I spent many a happy evening round my best mates' house (we are like brothers!) and being Indian his mum frequently had a curry of some sort on the go . although this is my take on a flavoursome and medium spiced curry, it is these evenings I am reminded of.

This recipe is dedicated to Harish and his mum.

Ingredients.

Chicken breast

1 large white onion

1 red pepper

1 stick celery

Baby corn

Mushrooms

Garlic puree

Fresh ginger

1 can coconut milk

Fresh coriander

Turmeric powder

Fresh lemongrass

Garam masala powder

All butter ghee

Chili flakes

Bay leaf

Cream or natural yoghurt


In a saucepan put a tablespoon of the ghee, add to it finely chopped onion a good squirt of garlic puree, chopped lemongrass and some grated ginger. Gently fry them together until the onion softens.

In a little cup put 1 tablespoon of turmeric and 1 tablespoon of Garam Masala, mix with a little water to form a paste (this stops it from burning) and add to the saucepan, stirring into the onion.

Now add in the can of coconut milk, this forms a base sauce for your curry.

De-seed and dice the red pepper into small pieces and add to the pan along with the baby corn, sliced mushrooms and diced celery.

Dice the chicken breast into quite large chunks, gently fry them off in a frying pan with a small amount of the Ghee, a little at a time and until it is starting to brown. As it is cooked, add it to your curry.

Finely chop the coriander and add to the saucepan along with a pinch of chili flakes and the bay leaf, giving it a good stir to mix the curry together, add cream or yoghurt (whichever you prefer). At this point taste the sauce, if it needs to be a stronger flavour you can add a teaspoon of curry powder (if you have some) or more garam masala.

Leave to simmer for around 1hr, making sure you stir the curry every now and then to stop it from sticking.

Before serving check the baby corn has cooked through, if not leave for a while longer.

I serve with easy boil in the bag rice, (use whatever rice you may have to hand) and a freshly made naan bread (see first section of this book)

# Chili con-steevie.

Sometimes I do like a nice hot and spicy chilli, I prefer it served with chips and cheese, but rice is just as good. A traditional chili uses kidney beans, as I don't like them, I have substituted them for something we all have in the cupboard!

Don't forget to put a toilet roll in the fridge for the next day after eating this!

Ingredients.

500g beef mince (10% fat content)

1 large white onion

2 cloves garlic

1 tin chopped plum tomatoes

1 tin baked beans

Tomato puree

Hot chili powder

Chili flakes

Salt & pepper

Dried mixed herbs

Mushrooms

Cheddar cheese

In a saucepan put a little oil (doesn't matter what type), finely chop the onion and garlic and add to the pan, gently fry until the onion softens and goes translucent.

Add the mince to the pan and cook until brown making sure the onion is mixed through the meat.

Now add the tin of tomatoes and stir thoroughly, add a good sprinkling of the mixed herbs, slice the mushrooms and also add to the pot.

Tip in the can of beans stirring through the mince mixture, add a pinch of the chili flakes, salt & pepper and 2 teaspoons of chili powder.

Simmer for 45mins with a lid on the saucepan, stirring frequently to combine all the flavours.

Use the tomato puree to thicken the sauce as required.

Meanwhile fry your chips in a deep fat fryer or air fryer, place oven chips in the oven, boil your rice (whatever you are accompanying the chili with)

Check the seasoning of your chili and serve. Grate some cheese over the top of your chili to finish.

Note.

If you prefer your chili not quite so hot, use normal chili powder and leave out the chili flakes.

Warning!!!!

It is a good idea to have a large glass of beer, milk or ice-cold water to hand!!

Any unused chili can be put into a plastic tub and kept in the fridge or freezer for a later date, but it will get hotter/ spicier as time goes on!

# Easy lasagne.

There are many different versions of this classic Italian dish. The traditional way is mainly about the pasta, the white sauce and ragu are not as important.

Served with garlic baguette and a simple Italian salad, it is a sure win to tantalise the taste buds.

This recipe uses a few "cheats" to make it easy to replicate but doesn't hold back on flavour.

## Ingredients.

Beef mince (low fat content)

1 red onion

1 clove garlic

1 tin chopped plum tomatoes

Fresh parsley

Fresh basil

Tomato puree

1 jar lasagne white sauce

Lasagne pasta sheets

Olive oil

Parmesan

Salt & pepper

Chop the onion and garlic and gently fry in a pan with olive oil until soft.

Add in the mince and cook until browned right through.

Combine the tomatoes into the pan with a pinch of salt & pepper.

Finally chop the basil and parsley and add along with a small squirt of tomato puree.

Simmer on a low heat to allow the ragu to sweeten and reduce down to a thick sauce. (add more tomato puree if needed)

Take off the heat and allow to cool.

Now it's time to build the lasagne, take an oven proof dish and build up layers.

First is a layer of the ragu, then a layer of the pasta sheets (make sure the pasta covers the whole of the ragu, it doesn't matter if the sheets overlap), next is a thin layer of the white sauce, then pasta, then ragu and so on until you have done a few layers.

The very last layer needs to be of the white sauce, then grate parmesan over the top of the whole dish.

Pre-heat the oven to 180'c and place the lasagne in the centre of the oven. Cook for approx. 25 mins, the top should go light brown. Take a sharp knife and check the pasta is cooked through by piercing thru the centre of the lasagne, it should slide in easily. If not, leave for a bit longer.

Time to serve, take a fish slice and use to remove a good slice of the lasagne out in one piece. Set on a plate alongside a simple salad (recipe for a tasty dressing is found in the first section of this book) and a couple of slices of garlic bread.

# Leek and potato soup.

Sometimes you just need a good hearty simple lunch, served with crusty bread on the side, this soup is tasty anytime of the day.

Ingredients.

2 large leeks

New potatoes

Maris piper potatoes

2 vegetable stock pots

1ltr water

Butter

Salt & pepper

Fresh parsley

In a large saucepan, melt a knob of butter. Slice the leeks and add to the saucepan, allow them to sweat a little before adding the water and stock pots.

Cut the new potatoes in half and add to the pan (leave on the skin), then peel and chop the rest of the potatoes and chop them into different sized chunks. Add them to the pan along with a pinch of salt & pepper.

Roughly chop up the parsley and add to your soup, give a good stir, place a lid over the top and allow to bubble for 1 1/2hrs.

Check that the potatoes are soft (some of the smaller chunks will have disintegrated and will thicken the soup) and serve with a large chunk of crusty bread.


That's it! Simple but tasty!

# Easy fish & new potatoes.

Have you ever wanted a nourishing meal but don't want all the hassle of standing for hours in the kitchen? This recipe is so easy, and only requires 1 saucepan and a metal colander.

Ingredients.

New potatoes

A piece of fish (could be any fillet you want, for this recipe I use salmon)

Butter

Fresh dill

Fresh parsley

Slice of lemon

Salt & pepper

Place your fish on a large piece of strong kitchen foil. Place a knob of butter on the top of the fish, finely chop the parsley and dill sprinkle on the top of the fish. Place the slice of lemon on top of everything and wrap the whole lot up in the foil to look like a Cornish pasty (make sure there is big space for heated air to circulate.

In a pan, place the potatoes and salted water. Put on the heat and wait until they start to boil. When the water is bubbling place a colander over the pan, place your parcel of fish in the colander and put a lid over the whole thing.

After about 20mins the potatoes should be cooked, and so is the fish!

Carefully open the foil and remove the fish onto a plate, drizzle with the butter left in the foil. Drain the potatoes and serve onto the plate.


Simple, easy to cook but very tasty! (and hardly any washing up!)

# Slow cooked honey & mustard roast gammon.

This is a great recipe if you are not in a hurry and have a slow cooker/ crock pot.

Anyone who has travelled through France and stopped for a meal in the services know they offer ham off the bone and chips! Delicious and succulent pieces of gammon. This will take you off on a journey of your taste buds.

Ingredients.

Joint of gammon ham

1 onion

100ml water

Honey

Dijon mustard

Place the joint of gammon in your slow cooker, cut the onion in half and place one half at each end of the joint. Pour the water down the side of the meat, then brush the top of the joint with mustard and honey.

Put the lid on the slow cooker and turn on the low setting for 6-8hrs

The steam from the water will slowly cook the ham, and the mustard and honey will form a lovely crust on the top.

For a really spectacular finish, you can take the joint out after 6hrs, place in a baking tray and brush again with honey, putting it in pre-heated oven at 180'c for about 20-30mins.

Carve slices off and serve.

Bon appetite

# Chicken noodle stir-fry.

Stir-fry is a quick and easy way to make a Chinese-style dish that is filling and tasty.

The trick is to have the wok (frying pan) very hot so that the ingredients cook very quickly.

You can add almost any vegetable to your stir-fry, but I stay with the usual candidates.

Ingredients.

Diced chicken breast

1 red onion

Red, green and yellow pepper

Mushrooms

Beansprouts

1 packet straight to wok egg noodles

Dark soy sauce

Worcester sauce

Fish sauce

Salt & pepper

Sweet chili sauce

You need to prepare all the ingredients before you start cooking as it is quite fast and furious once you get going.

Slice the onion into thin slices, do the same with the peppers (being careful to remove the seeds and white flesh), the mushrooms and any other veg you want to add. ( thin slices is the key to it cooking quickly)

Get your pan on the heat and up to a very high temperature, add a drizzle of oil (it should sizzle and smoke)

Throw in the chicken and stir, frying until it starts to brown, then add the onion, peppers, mushrooms and beansprouts. Stirring constantly.

Add a good splash of soy sauce, fish sauce and a dash of Worcester sauce, keep stirring

Add a pinch of salt & pepper.

Just before you serve, throw in the noodles and a splash of the sweet chili sauce, stir thoroughly in until the noodles distribute throughout the chicken.


Take off the heat and serve!

# Egg, cheese and potato pie.

A real crowd pleaser, simple ingredients, easy to prepare yet extremely filling and tasty.

I can't remember where I first had this, it wasn't the occasion that was memorable but the pie itself! Cutting into the mash piercing the egg to see it oozing out all over the plate …. divine!

It does call for a huge amount of mash potatoes but so worth the effort!

Ingredients.

Potatoes (good all-round spuds)

Butter

Cheddar cheese

Milk or cream

Eggs

1 large tomato

Salt & pepper

Peel and boil a large saucepan full of potatoes until they are soft.

Once cooked, drain the spuds and using a generous amount of butter, a good splash of milk or cream and a pinch of salt & pepper, give it all a good mashing until there are no lumps, just a big pot of creamy mashed spuds.

Take an oven-proof dish and spread a layer of the mash across the bottom (needs to come about halfway up the dish)

With the back of a tablespoon make several "wells" in the mash, they need to be big enough to easily house an egg without it spilling over the side. Then crack an egg (raw) into each of the wells.

Cut some of the cheese into chunks and place around the edges of your egg wells.

Carefully cover the cheese and eggs with the rest of your mash, take care not to break the yolk of your eggs.

Slice your tomato and place across the top of your mash (try to position the slices over the location of your egg wells) then grate more cheese over the whole of your dish.

Place in a pre-heated oven at 180'c for about 20-25mins (or until golden brown)

Then it's time to serve! Easy as pie.

# Beef stew and dumplings.

A stew of any kind is a winner in any household, this recipe uses the vegetables that you find in your veg rack, red wine and diced beef. Paired with fluffy dumplings, a guarantee to take you back to "granny's" house.

For the dumplings I use a shop bought dumpling mix (for quickness) but you can make your own if you wish.

Ingredients.

1 pack diced beef

Carrots

1 large leek

Parsnips

Baby new potatoes

Red wine (a good robust red like merlot)

1 rich beef stock pot

Gravy granules

1 tin of sweetcorn

1 pack of dumpling mix

Flour

Dried mixed herbs

Baby leaf spinach

1 tin of garden peas

1 stick of celery

Olive oil

For this you will need a large saucepan or soup pan.

There is no complicated process for this, more of a throw it all in and simmer approach, but a couple of ingredients need a little preparation first.

Slice the leeks, carrots, parsnips and celery into good sized pieces and add to your pan. Add a little drizzle of olive oil and start to sweat them down with a pinch of salt & pepper.

Add a good slug of the red wine, also a tablespoon of the mixed herbs.

Allow to simmer for 15 mins while you prepare the beef.

Cut off any fat from the beef and gently seal the chunks in a frying pan and drizzle of oil, then add them to your saucepan.

Add the potatoes (whole with skin left on)

Throw in the sweetcorn (with liquid), drain off the peas and add them as well.

Now it is time to add the stock pot, fill the tin from the peas with water and tip that in as well. (you need enough liquid to be about ¾ the height of your ingredients as the veg will shrink down as it cooks)

Lastly roughly chop the spinach and add to your pan.

Place a lid over the top and simmer for 1- 1 ½ hrs. Give the stew a good stir and add some of the gravy granules to thicken the liquid slightly.(not too much as you need it to be runny for the next step!)

Mix up the dumpling mix as per packet instructions, portion off into balls and roll them in the flour before adding to your pot. Cook for 20-25mins to allow the dumplings to cook and soak up some of the gravy.

Now it's time to eat!

# Cauliflower (and broccoli) cheese.

A nice cheesy/ creamy meal sometimes is all you need, include a crunchy topping and whether you eat it on its own or to accompany another dish, this recipe is sure to be a winner!

Ingredients.

Cauliflower (and broccoli)

500ml milk

4 tbsp plain flour

50g butter

100g grated cheddar cheese (mature or extra mature)

Grated red Leicester cheese

Breadcrumbs

For the sauce.

Pour 500ml milk into a large saucepan and add 4 tbsp plain flour and 50g butter.

Turn on the heat to medium and start to **whisk** the mixture. Keep whisking fast as the butter melts and the mixture comes to the boil – the flour will disappear, and the sauce will begin to thicken.

Whisk for another 2 mins while the sauce bubbles then stir in 100g grated strong cheddar cheese (or 50g grated cheddar, 50g crumbled blue cheese) until melted.

Place the cauliflower ( and broccoli ) into a pan and boil until soft. Drain off and place into an oven proof dish.

Pour over the cheese sauce so that all of the cauliflower has been covered.

Mix the breadcrumbs and red Leicester cheese together and spread over the top of your cauliflower.

Pre-heat the oven to 180'c, place your dish into the middle of the oven for approx. 20-25mins, take out and serve.

Note.

Shop bought packets of cheese sauce are great for an easy alternative, just mix with milk, heat and use!

# Flemish stew.

Anyone who has been to Belgium has probably at some point tried Flemish stew, called several different things (depending on where in Belgium you are), stoofvlees, carbonnade or a la flamande.

This is my version of the Belgian classic

<u>Ingredients.</u>

1 pack diced stewing steak

1 rich beef stock pot

1 white onion

1 bottle strong Belgian brown beer

Brown sugar

Silver skin onions

Flour

Salt & pepper

Fresh parsley

Fresh thyme

Cornflour

Place flour, salt & pepper into a bowl and toss the beef in the mixture until covered.

Fry in a little oil all the beef until slightly browned (do this in small batches).

After cooking each batch, add to a saucepan.

Once you have cooked all the beef, add the white onion (finely chopped), 2 teaspoons of brown sugar and a glug of the beer to the frying pan to soak up all the flavour and de-glaze the pan.

Add this to your saucepan along with the rest of the beer, the stockpot and the whole silver skin onions. Chop the parsley and thyme and add to the mix.

Now put a lid on the pot and simmer for 1-1 ½ hrs until the beef is tender. The sauce should have thickened up, if not, add a little cornflour to assist with the thickening.

And that's it, tasty, rich and satisfying.

Serve with plain boiled potatoes or chips and salad.

# Easy croque madam.

A great lunchtime snack, you can find these all over France. Normally served on flat sliced bread with a green salad or chips.

My version is on French baguette cut in half.

Ingredients.

1 part-baked baguette

Sliced ham

Cheese

Dijon mustard

Egg

Slice the baguette down the middle, spread a very thin amount of mustard on each piece, lay the ham over the mustard then cover with a grating of cheese. (as much as you like)

Pre-heat your oven to 180'c.Place your sandwich on a baking tray and put in the centre of your oven for 10mins

Take out and top with a fried egg.

And there it is, a croque madam.

# Easy pizza.

Sometimes you just want to sit down in front of the T.V. with a simple pizza. Why spend good money and the endless wait for the pizza delivery driver to arrive when using some basic ingredients and a little time, you can make your own for about £1.75 (including toppings!)

For this recipe I am using the slightly more expensive buffalo mozzarella, any cheese will do.

Ingredients.

(for the base)

350g plain flour

2 ¾ teaspoon baking powder

1 teaspoon salt

1 tablespoon oil

170ml water

(for the topping) (change for your preference)

1 jar passata

1 red onion

1 tin tuna

1 tomato

Fresh parsley

Fresh oregano

1 tub buffalo mozzarella

To make the base, put the flour, baking powder and salt into a bowl and mix together. Now add the oil and water, mix until all the flour is incorporated, and you end up with a firm but moist dough.(if it is sticky add a dusting of extra flour, if too dry add a tiny splash of water)

Place onto a floured chopping board and leave to rest for 5 mins. Kneed the dough for 2-3 mins until it is elastic.

Take ½ the dough and roll out to your desired thickness.

Turn on your oven to pre-heat to 180'c.

Now you can add your toppings, start by spreading the passata over the base making sure you have a good layer.

Then dot around the sliced onion, tuna, tomato, finely chopped parsley and oregano.

Finally rip the mozzarella into chunks and dot them over your pizza.

Place on a tray in the oven for about 15-20min or until it is cooked to your liking!

And that is all! Easy (and cheap) pizza. Just like mama used to make!!

## Kase spätzle. (Austrian mac & cheese)

Anyone who has visited the Vorarlberg in Austria will have at some point had the cheesy delight of Kase Spätzle. For me none can come close to the dish served by the Hotel Weisses Kreutz in Feldkirch.

Ingredients.

200g plain flour

3/4 teaspoon ground nutmeg

3/4 teaspoon salt

1/8 teaspoon pepper

3 eggs

90ml semi-skimmed milk

3 tablespoons butter

1 onion, sliced

175g grated Emmental cheese

Sift together flour, nutmeg, salt, and pepper. Beat eggs in a medium bowl. Alternately mix in milk and the flour mixture until smooth. Let stand for 30 minutes.

Bring a large pot of lightly salted water to the boil. Press spaetzle mixture through a colander or cheese grater into the water. When the spaetzle floats to the top of the water, remove it to a bowl with a slotted spoon. Mix in 2/3 of the cheese.

Melt butter in a large frying pan over medium-high heat. Add onion and cook until golden. Stir in spaetzle and remaining cheese until well blended. Remove from heat and serve immediately. Top with caramelised onions for an extra lift.

# **Apple crumble.**

I don't do many deserts, but this has been a firm favourite of mine ever since I was a small boy. (although I have adapted it slightly from the one my mum used to make)

I serve this with ready-made, Devon custard, just heated up in a pan, though it could be with cream.

Ingredients.

4 apples (eating apples, golden delicious, granny smiths or pink lady)

1 lemon

Brandy

Cinnamon powder

Flour

Butter (un-salted)

Demerara sugar

Put 50g of butter in a bowl and allow it to soften, with your hands mix in flour until the mixture resembles breadcrumbs, add a good handful of sugar and stir into the mix. Put to one side.

Take the cores out of the apples, peel and slice into thin slices, put into a separate bowl. Pour over the juice of the lemon and a good slug of brandy. Coat all the apples with the liquid.

In an oven proof dish, place the apples in layers, then tip over the juice from the bowl. Sprinkle a generous amount of cinnamon then cover with your crumble topping. Cook in a pre-heated oven at 180'c for 45mins and you are done!

Serve with whatever you like to accompany it.

Printed in Poland
by Amazon Fulfillment
Poland Sp. z o.o., Wrocław